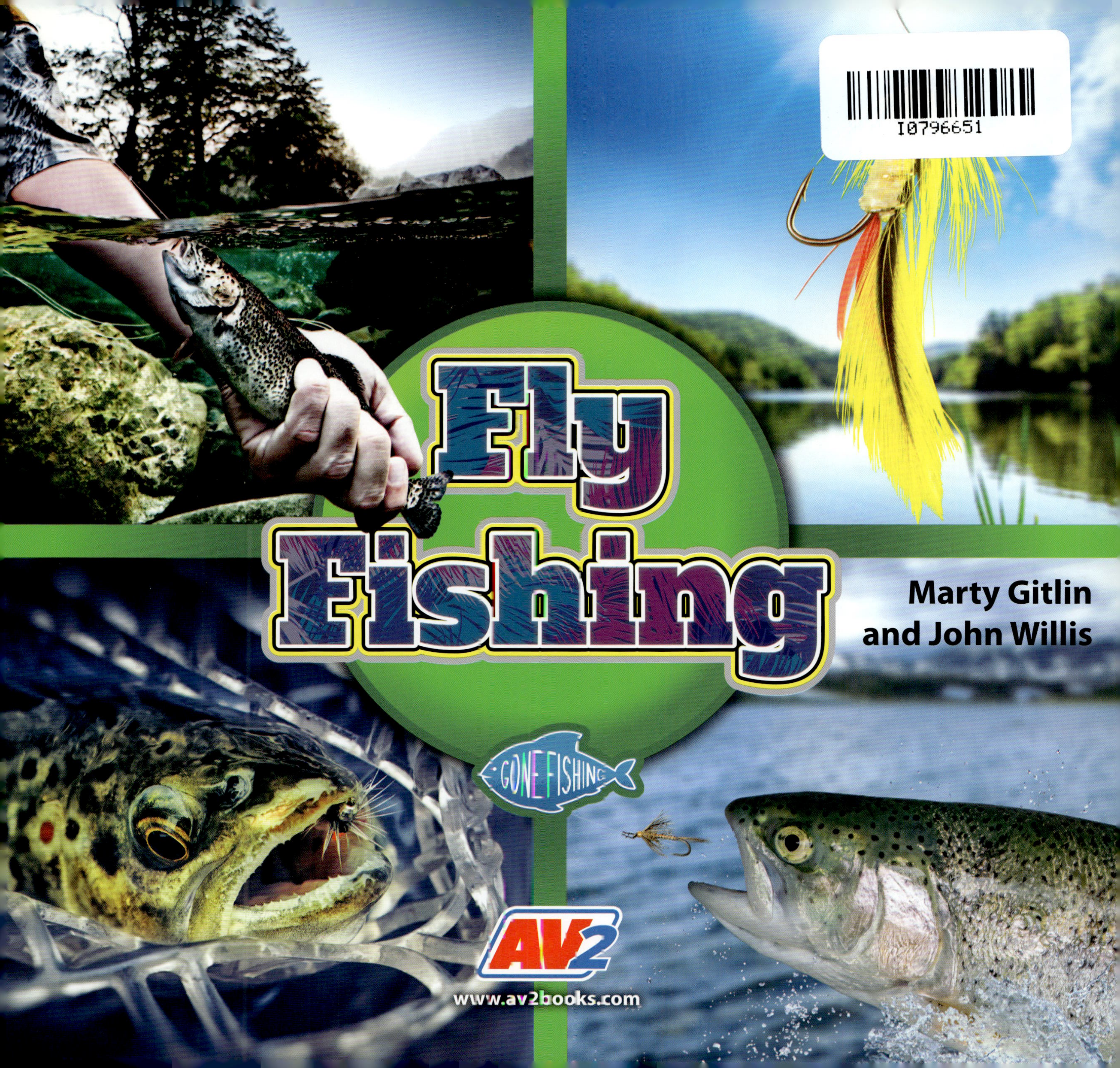

Fly Fishing
Marty Gitlin
and John Willis
GONE FISHING
AV2
www.av2books.com

**Step 1**
Go to **www.av2books.com**

**Step 2**
Enter this unique code

**JAGOZLTU0**

**Step 3**
Explore your interactive eBook!

AV2 is optimized for use on any device

## Your interactive eBook comes with...

**Audio**
Listen to the entire book read aloud

**Videos**
Watch informative video clips

**Weblinks**
Gain additional information for research

**Try This!**
Complete activities and hands-on experiments

**Key Words**
Study vocabulary, and complete a matching word activity

**Quizzes**
Test your knowledge

**Slideshows**
View images and captions

**View new titles and product videos at www.av2books.com**

# Fly Fishing

## Contents


2 AV2 Book Code
4 Fly Fishing
6 Fishing Tools
8 Types of Fish
10 Getting Wet
12 Catching a Fish
14 Saltwater Fly Fishing
16 Fly Fishing History
18 Fly Fishing Today
20 Fishing Responsibly
22 Fly Fishing Facts
24 Key Words

# Fly Fishing

Fly fishing is not fishing for flies! It is fishing using a hook called a fly.

Nearly five million Americans go fly fishing at least once a year.
The Alagnak River in Alaska is known as the prettiest fly fishing spot in America.

# Fishing Tools

People use fly rods, flies, and reels to catch fish.

Fly rods are longer than other fishing poles. They are used to cast fishing lines.

A fly fishing line has five knots. That helps fishers to control it.

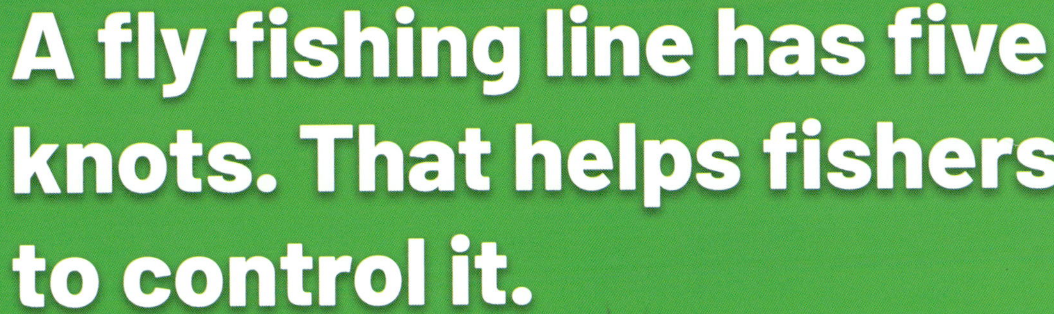

There are many kinds of flies.

# Types of Fish

Most fly fishers use flies that look like bugs.

Others use flies that look like tiny fish.

Trout and salmon are popular catches for freshwater fly fishers.

Fly fishers can catch marlin and tuna in salt water.

# Getting Wet

Fly fishers stand in shallow water. They keep casting in different spots to find fish.

Fly fishers cast flies just above the water. Fish do not see the line. All they see is the fly.

# Catching a Fish

When fish take the fly, they get caught. They will try to swim away.

Fly fishers let fish swim around. The fish get tired. Then, they are caught in nets or let go.

# Saltwater Fly Fishing

Saltwater fly fishers stand near the shore. They cast their fly into the water.

Saltwater fly fishers use stronger rods. This lets them catch bigger fish.

# Fly Fishing History

Early humans had to fish for food.

Fly fishing was one of the first ways that people fished for fun.

People began fly fishing nearly **2,000** years ago.

# Fly Fishing Today

Fly fishing tools have changed over time. Rods used to be wood. Today, they are graphite.

Old lines were silk or horsehair. New ones are made from nylon.

# Fishing Responsibly

Fly fishers should keep the water clean. They should take any trash home instead of throwing it in the water.

It is important to keep rivers and streams healthy. This makes sure there are enough fish for everyone.

# Fly Fishing Facts

## 17 Days

The average fisher spends about 17 days a year fishing.

The longest fly fishing rods are more than **10 feet** long.

# Top 5 countries for fly fishing

Iceland

Ireland

Canada

Norway

Russia

**The heaviest fish ever caught by a fly fisher was 385 pounds (175 kilograms).**

## Catch and Release

Most fly fishers just fish for fun. They return the fish they catch to the water.

# KEY WORDS

Research has shown that as much as 65 percent of all written material published in English is made up of 300 words. These 300 words cannot be taught using pictures or learned by sounding them out. They must be recognized by sight. This book contains 82 common sight words to help young readers improve their reading fluency and comprehension. This book also teaches young readers several important content words, such as proper nouns. These words are paired with pictures to aid in learning and improve understanding.

| Page | Sight Words First Appearance |
|---|---|
| 4 | a, for, is, it, not |
| 5 | Americans, as, at, go, in, known, once, the, year |
| 6 | and, are, lines, other, people, than, they, to, use |
| 7 | has, helps, kinds, many, of, that, there |
| 8 | like, look, most |
| 9 | can, water |
| 10 | different, find, keep |
| 11 | above, all, do, just, see |
| 12 | away, get, take, try, when, will |
| 13 | around, let, or, then |
| 14 | into, near, their |
| 15 | them, this |
| 17 | began, first, food, had, one, was, ways |
| 18 | be, changed, have, over, time |
| 19 | from, made, new, old, were |
| 20 | any, home, should |
| 21 | enough, important, makes, rivers |

| Page | Content Words First Appearance |
|---|---|
| 4 | flies, fly fishing, hook |
| 5 | Alagnak River, Alaska, spot |
| 6 | fish, fishing poles, fly rods, reels, tools |
| 7 | knots |
| 8 | bugs |
| 9 | marlin, salmon, trout, tuna |
| 10 | spots |
| 13 | nets |
| 17 | fun, humans |
| 18 | graphite, wood |
| 19 | horsehair, nylon, silk |
| 20 | trash |
| 21 | streams |

Published by AV2
350 5th Avenue, 59th Floor New York, NY 10118
Website: www.av2books.com



Library of Congress Control Number: 2019957570

ISBN 978-1-7911-2167-9 (hardcover)
ISBN 978-1-7911-2168-6 (softcover)
ISBN 978-1-7911-2169-3 (multi-user eBook)
ISBN 978-1-7911-2170-9 (single-user eBook)

Printed in Guangzhou, China
1 2 3 4 5 6 7 8 9 0 24 23 22 21 20

032020
100919

Art Director: Terry Paulhus Project Coordinator: John Willis



The publisher acknowledges Alamy, iStock, and Shutterstock as the primary image supplier for this title.